Letterland

Contents

T0352613

Level 1 - Student Book 2

Story ➡

Let's meet Harry Hat Man. Listen and repeat his name, sound and some words that start with his sound.

Track 69

hay

Hi. My name is Harry Hat Man.

2

Letter sound Harry Hat Man's sound is at the start of his name – **H**arry **H**at Man.

Sound

Listen and repeat Harry Hat Man's words. Complete the Keywords exercise in *Workbook 2*.

Workbook

Track 69

Harry Hat Man says, h.

He starts words like...

hat

house

hand

Move and chant!

Hhh, hhh, hhh.
Harry Hat Man! (x2)

 Multi-sensory   Hold your hand in front of your mouth and breathe onto it.

3

Song

Listen to the Alphabet Song. If you can, join in as you listen for the second time.

Track 71

Sing and point!

Harry Hat Man, he says hhh,
he says hhh, he says hhh.
Harry Hat Man, he says hhh,
he says hhh. (x2)
He says hhh. He says hhh.

I hate noise.
Please whisper,
'hhh...'

Workbook

Now you have completed all the sound activities in your *Student Book*, move on to your *Workbook* and complete the sound activities in there too!

Workbook

Uppercase ➤ Harry Hat Man does a handstand.

 # Let's finger-trace!

H h

Uppercase letters — You will see uppercase letters at the start of sentences, names or places. Practise writing the letters in *Workbook 2*.

 Workbook

5

Track 72

I love   I like   I don't like   I hate

Do you like cats?

Yes. I love cats.

Do you like dogs?

No. I hate dogs.

Now it's your turn!

Get Creative

Further activity suggestions can be found in the *Fix-it Phonics Teacher's Guide*.

Pair work

Practise in pairs. Take turns asking and answering questions. Ask about any of the objects you have learned so far.

Let's meet Bouncy Ben. Listen and repeat his name, sound and some words that start with his sound.

Track 73

Hello. My name is Bouncy Ben.

Letter sound Bouncy Ben's sound is at the start of his name – **B**ouncy **B**en.

Look for the things in the picture that start with his sound. Then complete the exercises in *Workbook 2*.

Workbook

Track 73

Bouncy Ben says, **b**.

He starts words like...

  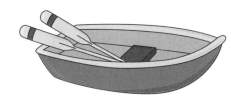

book **ball** **boat**

Do the action and say the rhythmic chant together!

Track 74

Move and chant!

B, b, b.
Bouncy Ben! (x2)

Multi-sensory Shoot your arms up for ears and wiggle them.

Song

Listen to the Alphabet Song. If you can, join in as you listen for the second time.

Track 75

Sing and point!

Bouncy Ben says, b, b.

Bouncy Ben says, b, b.

Bouncy Ben says, b, b.

Bouncy Ben says, b.

Bouncy Ben says, b.

B, b, b.

(x2)

b...

Workbook

Now you have completed all the sound activities in your *Student Book*, move on to your *Workbook* and complete the sound activities in there too!

Workbook

9

Uppercase ➤ Bouncy Ben balances a ball on his head.

 # Let's finger-trace!

B b

Uppercase letters You will see uppercase letters at the start of sentences, names or places. Practise writing the letters in *Workbook 2*.

 Workbook

Track 76

My family...

I have 1 sister.

dad

mum

sister

brother

I have 5 brothers.

Can you find them all in the big picture on page 7?

Now it's your turn!

Get Creative

Further activity suggestions can be found in the *Fix-it Phonics Teacher's Guide*.

Pair work Draw a picture of your family. Then describe your family to the class or to your partner.

Let's meet Firefighter Fred. Listen and repeat his name, sound and some words that start with his sound.

Forest Farm

Hi. My name is Firefighter Fred.

Letter sound Firefighter Fred's sound is at the start of his name – **F**irefighter **F**red.

12

Sound

Look for the things in the picture that start with his sound. Then complete the exercises in *Workbook 2*.

Workbook | Track 77

Firefighter Fred says, f.
He starts words like...

fish

frog

fire

Action

Do the action and say the rhythmic chant together!

Track 78

Move and chant!

Fff, fff.
Firefighter Fred! (x2)

Multi-sensory | Hold and point an imaginary hose towards an imaginary fire.

13

Song → Listen to the Alphabet Song. If you can, join in as you listen for the second time.

Track 79

Sing and point!

Firefighter Fred, fff.

Firefighter Fred, fff.

Firefighter Fred, fff.

He says, fff. (x3)

He says, fff.

He says, fff.

Workbook

Now you have completed all the sound activities in your *Student Book*, move on to your *Workbook* and complete the sound activities in there too!

Workbook

Uppercase ⟹ Firefighter Fred takes a deep breath and gets bigger.

 **Let's finger-trace!**

F f

Uppercase letters You will see uppercase letters at the start of sentences, names or places. Practise writing the letters in *Workbook 2*.

 Workbook

15

Talk time Fruit. Learning new words, asking questions and matching sounds.

Track 80

Who likes...?

| apple | banana | pear | orange | melon | strawberry |

I like fruit.

Who likes bananas?
Bouncy Ben likes bananas.

Now it's your turn!

Get Creative

Further activity suggestions can be found in the *Fix-it Phonics Teacher's Guide*.

Pair work Ask your partner who likes each fruit. Match one fruit to each of your Letterland friends. Change partners and repeat.

Let's meet Lucy Lamp Light. Listen and repeat her name, sound and some words that start with her sound.

Track 81

Hi. My name is Lucy Lamp Light.

Letter sound Lucy Lamp Light's sound is at the start of her name – **L**ucy **L**amp **L**ight.

Workbook · Track 81

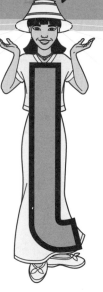

Lucy Lamp Light says, l.

She starts words like...

log   **leg**   **lion**

Move and chant!

Lll, lll.
Lucy Lamp Light! (x2)

  Multi-sensory · Touch your fingers above your head to suggest Lucy's hat.

Song ➤ Listen to the Alphabet Song. If you can, join in as you listen for the second time.

Track 83

Sing and point!

Lucy Lamp Light, she says, lll.

Lucy Lamp Light, she says, lll. (x3)

Workbook — Now you have completed all the sound activities in your *Student Book*, move on to your *Workbook* and complete the sound activities in there too!

Workbook

19

Uppercase

Lucy Lamp Light's legs get longer on the line.

Let's finger-trace!

L l

Uppercase letters You will see uppercase letters at the start of sentences, names or places. Practise writing the letters in *Workbook 2*.

Workbook

Talk time Home. Describing where you live and rooms in the house.

Track 84

I live in a lighthouse.

lighthouse house flat

bedroom

bed

bin

lounge

lamp

bathroom

kitchen

clock

duck tap

Pair work

Listen and point to the different rooms as you hear them.
Draw a picture of your house and describe it to your partner.

21

Best Friends

 Firefighter Fred's friend is Firefighter Frank.

off   coffee

 Lucy Lamp Light's friend is Linda Lamp Light.

doll   hill   smell

 Sammy Snake's friend is his sister Sally Snake.

hiss   kiss   glass

Word Building

Use the *Big Picture Code Cards* to build the words below or enjoy the Word Building activity on *Phonics Online*.

 Code Card

had	big	off	lap	hiss
him	back	fit	leg	mess
hot	bad	fun	log	boss
hut	bag	fig	bell	kiss
hop	bed	fog	fill	Tess
hit	bug	puff	doll	
hat	bus	fan	sell	
hug	bucket	fat	laptop	

Red words = Keywords previously covered

Word Building

Focus on blending and segmenting the sounds. Use the techniques described in the *Fix-it Phonics Teacher's Guide*.

Read the stories in *Phonics Readers 5*, featuring the phonic elements in this *Student Book*.

A hat for a pet

Focus on: h as in hen

Comprehension

Point to the correct answer.

1. What does Harry have for his pets?

◯ hats   ☐ pens

Ben and the cub

Focus on: b as in bat

2. What did Ben have in his bag?

◯ a bag   ☐ a bun

Huff and puff!

Focus on: f as in fan

3. Listen and complete the sentence. Fred and Frank are...

◯ fat   ☐ fit

Leg rest

Focus on: l as in leg

4. Did Lucy get to rest her leg on the log?

◯ yes   ☐ no

Workbook

Workbook

Now complete the writing and listening exercises in your *Workbook*.

Pair work

When you have read the stories, the teacher will read the questions. Work in pairs or small groups to read and point to the correct answers.

Story

Let's meet Jumping Jim. Listen and repeat his name, sound and some words that start with his sound.

Track 86

Hello. My name is Jumping Jim.

Letter sound — Jumping Jim's sound is at the start of his name – Jumping Jim.

Sound ▶ Look for the things in the picture that start with his sound. Then complete the exercises in *Workbook 2*.

Workbook

 Track 86

Jumping Jim says, j.
He starts words like...

jet   **juice**   **jam**

Action ▶ Do the action and say the rhythmic chant together!

 Track 87

Move and chant!

J, j, j. J, j, j.
Jumping Jim!   (x2)

Multi-sensory ⚑ Pretend you are juggling a set of imaginary balls.

25

Song Listen to the Alphabet Song. If you can, join in as you listen for the second time.

Track 88

Sing and point!

j

Jumping Jim says j, j.

Jumping Jim says j.

Jumping Jim says j, j.

Jumping Jim says j.

J, j, j, j. Jumping Jim says j, j.

Jumping Jim says j, j.

j... Jumping Jim says j. (x2)

Workbook Now you have completed all the sound activities in your *Student Book*, move on to your *Workbook* and complete the sound activities in there too! Workbook

Uppercase Jumping Jim takes a deep breath and gets so big his head and his juggling balls are hidden by the clouds!

 Let's finger-trace!

J j

Uppercase letters You will see uppercase letters at the start of sentences and starting names or places. Practise writing the letters in *Workbook 2*.

27

jacket   T-shirt   dress   hat

Track 89

1

Can I have a red jacket, please?

2

Here you are.

3

Thank you.

4

Now it's your turn!

See *Fix-it Phonics Teacher's Guide* for more ideas!

Role-play Pretend you are in a shop asking for clothes. Play the roles of the shop assistant and customer. Describe the colour, too!

28

Story ➡️

Let's meet Vicky Violet. Listen and repeat her name, sound and some words that start with her sound.

Track 90

Hi. My name is Vicky Violet.

Letter sound Vicky Violet's sound is at the start of her name – **V**icky **V**iolet.

29

Sound ⟩ Look for the things in the picture that start with her sound. Then complete the exercises in *Workbook 2*.

Workbook  Track 90

Vicky Violet says, V.
She starts words like...

van   vegetables   vet

Action ⟩ Do the action and say the rhythmic chant together!

Track 91

Move and chant!

Vvv, vvv.
Vicky Violet! (x2)

 **Multi-sensory** Hold your hands together in a V-shape.

30

Song

Listen to the Alphabet Song. If you can, join in as you listen for the second time.

Sing and point!

Vicky Violet, Vicky Violet,

says vvv, says vvv.

Vicky Violet, Vicky Violet,

says vvv, says vvv. (x2)

 Now you have completed all the sound activities in your *Student Book*, move on to your *Workbook* and complete the sound activities in there too!

Workbook

31

Uppercase | Vicky Violet takes a deep breath and her letter gets bigger.

 Let's finger-trace!

Uppercase letter You will see uppercase letters at the start of sentences and starting names or places. Practise writing the letters in *Workbook 2*.

Workbook

carrots
potatoes
peppers
onions

cabbages
tomatoes
mushrooms

There is 1 carrot
There are 2 carrots

1

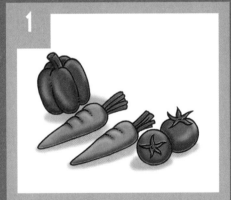

2

3

Now it's your turn!

See *Fix-it Phonics Teacher's Guide* for more ideas!

I love vegetables!

Pair work   Learn the names of the vegetables and then describe the three pictures to your partner. "There is 1 pepper, there are 2 carrots,..."

33

Let's meet Walter Walrus. Listen and repeat his name, sound and some words that start with his sound.

Track 94

Hi. My name is Walter Walrus.

Letter sound — Walter Walrus's sound is at the start of his name – **W**alter **W**alrus.

Sound

Look for the things in the picture that start with his sound. Then complete the exercises in *Workbook 2*.

Workbook

Track 94

Walter Walrus says, W.

He starts words like...

water   **watch**   **window**

Action Do the action and say the rhythmic chant together!

Track 95

Move and chant!

Www, www.
Walter Walrus! (x2)

Multi-sensory Flick both hands up and outwards so your arms form a W-shape.

35

Song Listen to the Alphabet Song. If you can, join in as you listen for the second time.

Sing and point!

W

Walter Walrus, he says w.

Walter Walrus, he says w.

Walter Walrus, he says w.

He says, w. (x3)

Workbook Now you have completed all the sound activities in your *Student Book*, move on to your *Workbook* and complete the sound activities in there too!

Workbook

Uppercase ⟶ Walter Walrus takes a deep breath and gets bigger.

 # Let's finger-trace!

W w

Uppercase letter You see uppercase letters at the start of sentences and starting names or places. Practise writing the letters in *Workbook 2*.

 Workbook

37

Track 97

 sunny  cloudy rainy  windy

How's the weather today?

1

2

3

4

Oral language

Look at the pictures and describe the weather.
"It's cloudy." "It's rainy." "It's windy." "It's sunny."

Hello. My name is Fix-it Max.

Letter sound Fix-it Max's sound is at the end of his name – Fix-it Max.

39

Sound

Look for the things in the picture that end with his sound. Then complete the exercises in *Workbook 2*.

 Workbook

 Track 98

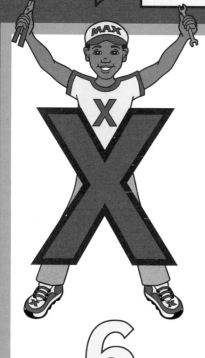

Fix-it Max says, **X**.

He ends words like...

6

six

box

fox

Action

Do the action and say the rhythmic chant together!

 Track 99

Move and chant!

X, x, x.

Fix-it Max! (x2)

Multi-sensory Cross your arms on your chest to make an X-shape.

Sing and point!

  **X**

Fix-it Max says x, x.

Fix-it Max says x.

Fix-it Max says x, x.

Fix-it Max says x.

Fix-it Max, Fix-it Max.

x...

Fix-it Max says x, x.

Fix-it Max says x, x.

Fix-it Max says x. (x2)

Workbook Now you have completed all the sound activities in your *Student Book*, move on to your *Workbook* and complete the sound activities in there too!

Workbook

41

Uppercase Fix-it Max takes a deep breath and gets bigger.

 **Let's finger-trace!**

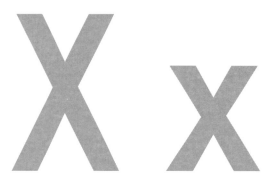

Uppercase letter You will see uppercase letters at the start of sentences, names or places. Practise writing the letters in your *Workbook 2*.

Workbook

Talk time Let's play. Invite your friends to do things with you.

point

count

smell

wave

smile

sit

stand

shout

be quiet

listen

Let's wave. Let's count. Let's ride a bike.

Yes, okay.   Okay.   No, thanks.

Pair work Work in pairs. Invite your partner to do each of the activities.
If they say "yes", pretend to do the activity. If they say "no", don't.

43

Oral blending. Make the individual sounds.
Then start to blend the sounds to make the word.

j a m

j a m

jam

Sound Slide

Try using the Sound Slide.
For further details see
Fix-it Phonics Teacher's Guide.

Phonics Online

Try building the words with *Phonics Online*.

jam	win
jet	web

Red words = Keywords previously covered

44

Word Building

Blend the sounds or 'Live Spell' some of these words.
You could also learn the meaning of all the words here.

Read the stories in *Phonics Readers 6*, featuring the phonic elements in this *Student Book*.

Letterland Phonics Readers **6**

Just jump!
and other stories

Focus on:
• j as in jet
• v as in van
• w as in wig
• x as in box

Four decodable stories

Comprehension

Point to the correct answer.

Just jump!

Focus on: j as in jet

1. Where does Ben work?

○ On a bus.   ☐ In bed.

At the Vet's

Tricky words: this, to, h, me

Focus on: v as in van

2. What animals does Vicky take to the vet?

○ a dog   ☐ a dog
a duck   a cat
a frog   a duck

Wet

Tricky words: said, what, of

Focus on: w as in wig

3. What did Dippy Duck not want to get wet?

○ a doll   ☐ a duck

Can he fix it?

Tricky words: you

Focus on: x as in box

4. What did Max fix for Jim?

○ relax   ☐ a jet

Workbook

Now complete the writing and listening exercises in your *Workbook*.

Workbook

Pair work
When you have read the stories, the teacher will read the questions. Work in pairs or small groups to read and point to the correct answers.

Let's meet Yellow Yo-yo Man. Listen and repeat his name, sound and some words that start with his sound.

Track 103

Hello. I'm Yellow Yo-yo Man.

Letter sound

Yellow Yo-yo Man's sound is at the start of his name – **Y**ellow **Y**o-yo Man.

Look for the things in the picture that start with his sound. Then complete the exercises in *Workbook 2*.

Yellow Yo-yo Man says, Y.
He starts words like...

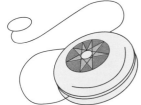
yo-yo

yellow

yogurt

**Action** Track 104

Do the action and say the rhythmic chant together!

Move and chant!
Y, y, y, y.
Yellow Yo-yo Man! (x2)

 Multi-sensory — Move your hand up and down as if playing with a yo-yo.

47

Song Listen to the Alphabet Song. If you can, join in as you listen for the second time.

Sing and point!

Yo-yo Man says yyy,
says yyy, says yyy.
Yo-yo Man says yyy.
Yo-yo Man says yyy.
Yo-yo Man says yyy.
Yo-yo Man says yyy. (x2)

Workbook Now you have completed all the sound activities in your *Student Book*, move on to your *Workbook* and complete the sound activities in there too!

Workbook

Uppercase ➤ Yellow Yo-yo Man steps up on to the line.

Let's finger-trace!

Uppercase letter You will see uppercase letters at the start of sentences, names or places. Practise writing the letters in *Workbook 2*.

Workbook

49

Can a dog jump?   Yes / No

Can a man hop?   Yes / No

Can a van hop?   Yes / No

Can a fox get in a box?   Yes / No

Can a cat get on a frog?   Yes / No

Can a frog jump?   Yes / No

Now it's your turn!

Get Creative

Further activity suggestions can be found in the *Fix-it Phonics Teacher's Guide*.

Oral language

Work in pairs to read and answer the questions.
Read the questions three times to improve fluency.

Let's meet Zig Zag Zebra. Listen and repeat her name, sound and some words that start with her sound.

Track 106

Hi. My name is Zig Zag Zebra.

Letter sound — Zig Zag Zebra's sound is at the start of her name – **Zig Zag Zebra.**

Sound

Look for the things in the picture that start with her sound. Then complete the exercises in *Workbook 2*.

Workbook  Track 106

Zig Zag Zebra says, Z.

She starts words like...

zero

zip

zoo

Action Track 107

Do the action and say the rhythmic chant together!

Move and chant!

Zzz, zzz,

Zig Zag Zebra! (x2)

Multi-sensory Rest your head against your hands to mime falling asleep.

Song ➤ Listen to the Alphabet Song. If you can, join in as you listen for the second time.

Track 108

Sing and point!

 **Z**

Zig Zag Zebra zzz.

Zig Zag Zebra zzz.

Zig Zag Zebra zzz.

Zig Zag Zebra, she says zzz.

Zzz. (x2)

zzz...

Uppercase → Zig Zag Zebra takes a deep breath and gets bigger.

 **Let's finger-trace!**

Z z

Uppercase letter You will see uppercase letters at the start of sentences, names or places. Practise writing the letters in *Workbook 2*.

Workbook

Sometimes, Zig Zag Zebra's best friend helps at the end of words. She is called Zoe Zebra.

Zig Zag Zebra   ## Zoe Zebra

buzz

fizz

Listen and point to the correct Letterlanders.
They like animals that start with their sound.

Track 109

You know...

lion

elephant

zebra

56

Listen & learn Look for and point to all the different animals in the zoo.
Point to them again as you listen and learn their names.

Track 110

Story ➡️

Let's meet Quarrelsome Queen. Listen and repeat her name, sound and some words that start with her sound.

Track 111

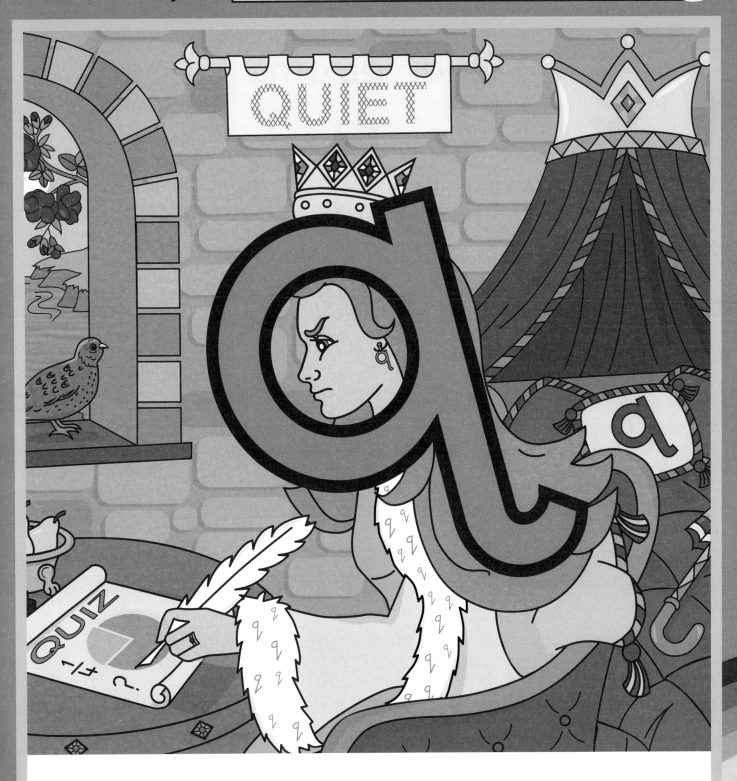

Hello, I'm Quarrelsome Queen.

Letter sound Quarrelsome Queen's sound is at the start of her name – **Qu**arrelsome **Qu**een.

57

Sound ▶ Look for the things in the picture that start with her sound. Then complete the exercises in *Workbook 2*.

Workbook  Track 111

Quarrelsome Queen says, **qu**.

She starts words like...

quarter question quilt

Action ▶ Do the action and say the rhythmic chant together!

 Track 112

Move and chant!

Qu, qu, qu, qu.

Quarrelsome Queen! (x2)

 Multi-sensory ▷ Point your index finger as if asking for 'Quiet!'.

Song Listen to the Alphabet Song. If you can, join in as you listen for the second time.

Track 113

Sing and point!

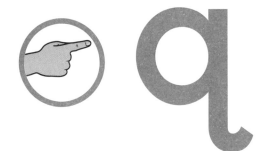

Quarrelsome Queen says qu, qu.
Quarrelsome Queen says qu, qu.
Quarrelsome Queen says qu, qu.
Quarrelsome Queen says qu. (x3)

Workbook

Now you have completed all the sound activities in your *Student Book*, move on to your *Workbook* and complete the sound activities in there too!

59

Uppercase → Quarrelsome Queen sits in her Quiet Room.

Let's finger-trace!

Q q

Uppercase letter You will see uppercase letters at the start of sentences, names or places. Practise writing the letters in *Workbook 2*.

Workbook

Quick quiz ▷ Listen to the queen as she asks some questions.

Track 114

Listen to Quarrelsome Queen's quick quiz questions.

1. What colour is a banana?

2. What colour is a tomato?

3. Is this a cat?

 | yes | no |

4. Is this a dog?

 | yes | no |

5. How many hats?

 | 6 | 3 |

6. How many socks?

 | 2 | 5 |

7. Is it sunny?

 | yes | no |

8. Is it rainy?

 | yes | no |

Listen — Listen to the question and point to the correct answer.
You could work in pairs or small groups.

61

Quick Dash

Now you know all the **a-z** sounds and shapes. Use your *Big Picture Code Cards* to quickly revise them.

Code Card

Revision Go through the whole alphabet slowly at first. Then get faster and faster. Use a stopwatch to record the time it takes!

Workbook

Story

Noisy Nick and Golden Girl make a different sound when they are together. Listen.

Track 117

I'm Noisy Nick. I say, 'nnn'.

I'm Golden Girl. I say, 'g'.

Two letters together!

When Noisy Nick and Golden Girl get together they are so happy they sing, "ng!".

Phonics Online

Meet Noisy Nick and Golden Girl on *Phonics Online*. Listen to their sound and sing along to the animated song.

2 letters: 1 sound Golden Girl and Noisy Nick sing 'ng' when they are together in the middle or end of words.

63

Listen to the story about what happens when Noisy Nick and Golden Girl come together in a word.

Noisy Nick and Golden Girl

Multi-sensory Pretend to be Noisy Nick or Golden Girl humming and singing.

Find these items in the picture. Listen for the **'ng'** sound at the end of the words.

Track 119

sing

king

ring

wing

painting

New words When you have finished this page, do the Keywords exercise in *Workbook 2*.

Workbook

65

r i ng

ring

Sound Slide

Try using the Sound Slide.
For further details see
Fix-it Phonics Teacher's Guide.

Read ➤ Now try to read this full sentence. Read it more than once to
gain fluency.

The king rings the bell.

66
Song Optional: Listen to Noisy Nick and Golden Girl's song. If you can, join
in with the chorus when you listen for the second time.

Track 120

Read the stories in *Phonics Readers 7*, featuring the phonic elements in this *Student Book*.

Yo-yo Man's yams

Focus on: y as in yes

Comprehension

Point to the correct answer.

1. What animal did the King and Queen meet in this story?

◯ a yeti   ☐ a yak

Zig, zag

Focus on: z as in zip

2. What sound does a bee make?

◯ buzz   ☐ zig zag

A quick quiz

Focus on: qu as in quiz

3. What expression is a way to say you 'give up'?

◯ I quack.   ☐ I quit.

Ding dong

Focus on: ng as in ring

4. Who rings the bell?

◯ the king   ☐ the duck

Workbook

Workbook

Now complete the writing and listening exercises in your *Workbook*.

Pair work

When you have read the stories, the teacher will read the questions. Work in pairs or small groups to read and point to the correct answers.

 I'm Annie Apple. I say, a.

 I'm Eddy Elephant. I say, e.

 I'm Impy Ink. I say, i.

 I'm Oscar Orange. I say, o.

 I'm Uppy Umbrella. I say, u.

Let's meet ▶ The Vowel Men. Listen to the Vowel Men. Point to each Vowel Man as he says his name.

Long vowels The Vowel Men say their names in words: **a e i o u**

68

Let's meet Mr A. He says his name, a, in words.
Listen to Mr A, the Apron Man.

Track
124

Hello. I'm Mr A, the Apron Man.

Look Look for the things in the scene that start with Mr A, saying his name.

Track 125

Good day. I'm Mr A. I say my name, **a**.

I start words like...

acorn

alien

apron

Action Wave your hand and shout '**a**' if you hear Mr A's name!

Track 126

Listen and shout!

apple   alien   cat   duck   age

apron   Asia   cake   gate

Song Listen to the Mr A verse. Listen first, then join in with just the '**a**...' sound. Finally sing the whole song together.

Track 127

70

Vowel Sounds Listen and repeat Mr A's words. Then complete the Keywords exercise in *Workbook 2*.

Workbook

Let's meet Mr E. He says his name, **e**, in words.
Listen to Mr E, the Easy Magic Man.

Hello. I'm Mr E, the Easy Magic Man.

Look | Look for the things in the scene that start with Mr E, saying his name.

Sound

Mr E, the Easy Magic Man, just says his name.

Greetings. I'm Mr E. I say my name, e.

I start words like...

eat

east

eagle

Action

Wave your hand and shout 'e' if you hear Mr E's name!

Listen and shout!

sheep	ink	easy	egg	she
hat	eat	he	eel	

Song

Listen to the Mr E verse. Listen first, then join in with just the 'e...' sound. Finally sing the whole song together.

Vowel Sounds

Listen and repeat Mr E's words. Then complete the Keywords exercise in *Workbook 2*.

 Workbook

Story

Let's meet Mr I. He says his name, i, in words.
Listen to Mr I, the Ice Cream Man.

Track
132

Ice cold lollies and fine Ice cream

Hello. I'm Mr I, the Ice Cream Man.

Look Look for the things in the scene that start with Mr I, saying his name.

73

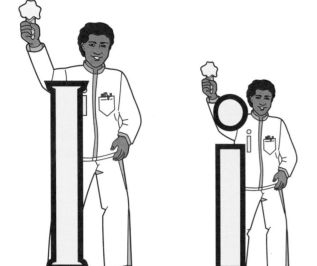

Hi. I'm Mr I.
I say my name, i.
I start words like...

ice cream

island

iron

Action

Wave your hand and shout 'i' if you hear Mr I's name!

Listen and shout!

island   ice   box   find   kind
insect   like   ice cream   iron

Song

Listen to the Mr I verse. Listen first, then join in with just the 'i...' sound. Finally sing the whole song together.

Vowel Sounds

Listen and repeat Mr I's words. Then complete the Keywords exercise in *Workbook 2*.

Workbook

Story ➡ Let's meet Mr O. He says his name, **o**, in words.
Listen to Mr O, the Old Man.

Track
136

Hello. I'm Mr O, the Old Man.

Look Look for the things in the scene that start with Mr O, saying his name.

Hello. I'm Mr O. I say my name, O.

I start words like...

open

old

ocean

Action Wave your hand and shout 'o' if you hear Mr O's name!

Listen and shout!

stop	open	cold	bed	only
on	old	ocean	over	

Song Listen to the Mr O verse. Listen first, then join in with just the 'o...' sound. Finally sing the whole song together.

Vowel Sounds Listen and repeat Mr O's words. Then complete the Keywords exercise in *Workbook 2*.

Workbook

Story

Let's meet Mr U. He says his name, **u**, in words.
Listen to Mr U, the Uniform Man.

Track
140

Hello. I'm Mr U, the Uniform Man.

Look   Look for the things in the scene that start with Mr U, saying his name.

77

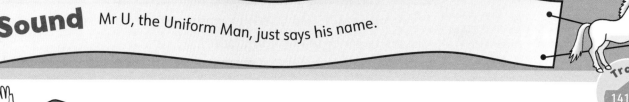

How do you do?

I'm Mr U.

I say my name, u.

I start words like...

uniform   unicycle   unicorn

Action Wave your hand and shout '**u**' if you hear Mr U's name!

Listen and shout!

uniform	use	unicycle	tune	
dog	cup	university	music	cube

Song Listen to the Mr U verse. Listen first, then join in with just the '**u**...' sound. Finally sing the whole song together.

Vowel Sounds Listen and repeat Mr U's words. Then complete the Keywords exercise in *Workbook 2*.

 Workbook

Song ⟶ Listen and sing along to the complete Vowel Men Song.

 Track 144

Listen to the song!

I am a Vowel Man. My name is Mr A.
I wear an apron, an apron everyday.
All five of us are Vowel Men,
and I am Mr A!
All five of us are Vowel Men,
and I am Mr A!

I am a Vowel Man. My name is Mr E.
My magic tricks are marvellous to see.
All five of us are Vowel Men,
and I am Mr E!
All five of us are Vowel Men,
and I am Mr E!

I am a Vowel Man. My name is Mr I.
I sell ice cream for you
to come and buy.
All five of us are Vowel Men,
and I am Mr I!
All five of us are Vowel Men,
and I am Mr I!

I am a Vowel Man. My name is Mr O.
I am an old man but I'm still full of go.
All five of us are Vowel Men,
and I am Mr O!
All five of us are Vowel Men,
and I am Mr O!

I am a Vowel Man. My name is Mr U.
I have a uniform, a uniform that's blue.
All five of us are Vowel Men,
and I am Mr U!
All five of us are Vowel Men,
and I am Mr U!

We're glad to meet you.
We hope you understand:
you are all welcome
here in Letterland!
Oh, all of you are welcome
here in Letterland.

If you make all the consonant sounds correctly then blending sounds should cause no difficulties.

1. Listen to the Audio.

2. Point to the keywords.

3. Join in with the chant.

Optional: Listen to the song on Phonics Online.

Blend

It's important to understand that these are not new sounds, they are sounds the children already know, simply blended together.

If you make all the consonant sounds correctly then blending sounds should cause no difficulties.

Track 149

Bouncy Ben and Lucy Lamp Light blend together to start words like...

b	⟶	lll	⟶	bl
blue		black		blend

Track 150

Clever Cat and Lucy Lamp Light blend together to start words like...

c	⟶	lll	⟶	cl
clap		clock		clown

Song

There are songs for all the blends on *Phonics Online*. Don't try to understand all the song words, just listen out for the blended sounds.

Track 151

Firefighter Fred and Lucy Lamp Light blend together to start words like...

fff → lll → fl

flag   flowers   flame

Track 152

Golden Girl and Lucy Lamp Light blend together to start words like...

g → lll → gl

glue   gloves   glass

Track 153

Peter Puppy and Lucy Lamp Light blend together to start words like...

p → lll → pl

plant   plate   plug

Track 154

Sammy Snake and Lucy Lamp Light blend together to start words like...

sss   lll   sl

slide   sleep   slug

Listen Listen and join in with the audio. The simple chants are easy to say, so everyone can participate.

Track 155

Bouncy Ben and Red Robot blend together to start words like...

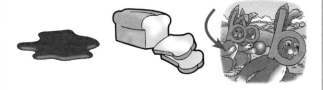

b	→	rrr	→	br
brown		bread		brother

Track 156

Clever Cat and Red Robot blend together to start words like...

c	→	rrr	→	cr
crab		cry		crown

Track 157

Dippy Duck and Red Robot blend together to start words like...

d	→	rrr	→	dr
drum		dress		drink

Track 158

Firefighter Fred and Red Robot blend together to start words like...

fff	→	rrr	→	fr
frog		fruit		friends

Workbook

After you have looked at these pages, complete the activities for the blends you have learned so far in *Workbook 2*.

Workbook

Track 159

Golden Girl and Red Robot
blend together to start words like...

g → rrr → gr

green   grass   grapes

Track 160

Peter Puppy and Red Robot
blend together to start words like...

p → rrr → pr

press   price   present

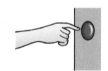

Track 161

Talking Tess and Red Robot
blend together to start words like...

t → rrr → tr

tree   train   triangle

Song There are songs for all the blends on *Phonics Online*. Don't try to understand all the song words, just listen out for the blended sounds.

Track 162

Sammy Snake and Clever Cat blend together to start words like...

sss ➡ c ➡ sc

scarf   school   scales

Track 163

Sammy Snake and Kicking King blend together to start words like...

sss ➡ k ➡ sk

skip   ski   skirt

Track 164

Sammy Snake and Peter Puppy blend together to start words like...

sss ➡ p ➡ sp

spin   spoon   space

Track 165

Sammy Snake and Talking Tess blend together to start words like...

sss ➡ t ➡ st

stop   stamp   star

Blends

After you have looked at these pages, complete the activities for the blends you have learned so far in *Workbook 2*.

Workbook

 **Sammy Snake and Munching Mike blend together to start words like...**

sss → mmm → sm

smell   smile   small

  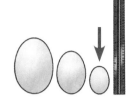

 **Sammy Snake and Noisy Nick blend together to start words like...**

sss → nnn → sn

snake   snow   snail

 **Sammy Snake and Walter Walrus blend together to start words like...**

sss → www → sw

swim   swing   sweets

 Sounds   Now you have learned what happens when sounds blend together. Complete *Workbook 2* blends pages, then let's try reading some blended words!

Let's read!

A frog sits on a clock.   Clap!   It jumps off.

A frog sits on a flag.   Clap!   It jumps off.

A frog sits on a plant.   Clap!   It jumps off.

A frog sits on a slug.   Clap!   It jumps off.

Fluency Read the sentences slowly at first. Then read them again faster. Try to add expression and add the clap as an action too!

Read the stories in *Phonics Readers 8*, featuring the phonic elements in this *Student Book*.

Comprehension

Point to the correct answer.

A robin on a clock

Focus on: bl, cl, fl, gl, pl as in *block, clock, flag, glad, plug*

1. What colour is the clock the robin sits on?

○ red ☐ black

Drip, drip, drop!

Focus on: br, cr, dr, fr, gr, tr as in *brick, crab, drip, frog, grin, track*

2. What does Golden Girl see on a rock?

○ a bug ☐ a frog

It is hot!

Focus on: sl, sp, st, sw as in *slip, spot, stuck, swim*

3. Why is Sam sad?

○ He is hot. ☐ He has spots.

4. What happened to Max?

Skid, smack!

Focus on: sk, sl, sm, sn, st as in *skate, slip, smash, snap, stuck*

○ He hit a rock and got a cut.

☐ He hit a rock and got a stamp.

Workbook

Now complete the writing and listening exercises in your *Workbook*.

Workbook

Pair work

When you have read the stories, the teacher will read the questions. Work in pairs or small groups to read and point to the correct answers.